Little Books 123

by Christine E. McCormick

Good Year Books

Parsippany, New Jersey

Acknowledgments

The author thanks Jan Eldridge for her help with the first draft's illustrations.

Good Year Books

are available for most basic curriculum subjects plus many enrichment areas. For more Good Year Books, contact your local bookseller or educational dealer. For a complete catalog with information about other Good Year Books, please write:

Good Year Books
An imprint of Pearson Learning
299 Jefferson Road
Parsippany, New Jersey 07054-0480
1-800-321-3106
www.pearsonlearning.com

Design and Illustration: Street Level Studio

ISBN   0-673-58659-6

Table of Contents

Preface

Little Books 1, 2, 3 contains 22 reproducible, easy-to-recite, high-interest books for children who are learning to count and to recognize numerals for the numbers 1 through 20. The books provide a print context that encourages practice with counting and understanding of number. The first twenty books focus on one number and presents the numeral in a brief text about that number. These six-page Little Books provide an easy-to-remember text with child-friendly supporting illustrations. The last two Little Books let the child "Be the Illustrator." Children practice their counting skills by drawing the correct number of items to match the text.

Introduction

Learning to count to 20, to recognize the numeral for each of the numbers 1 through 20, and associating quantity with each number are components of most kindergarten curricula. *Little Books 1, 2, 3* fosters practice with counting and understanding of number and with recognizing the numerals for the numbers 1 through 20.

Any or all of the books may be used, either as a part of the curriculum for all children or as a supplement for individual or small groups of children.

Styled upon the successful format of *Little Books* (published in 1990 by Good Year Books) and *Little Books from A to Z* (published in 1998 by Good Year Books), *Little Books 1, 2, 3* presents a few words of text on each page with an illustration that depicts the text. They are intended to be introduced during number instruction and then given to each child to read, count, color, and keep.

Little Books 1, 2, 3 is intended to supplement other class activities with numbers; the Little Books encourage practice with counting and matching the numeral to quantity. Each book presents numbers in context that emphasizes counting real things from children's everyday experiences.

Procedures

Getting Ready for the Lessons

Present *Little Books 1, 2, 3* in the same sequence that you introduce or review the numbers 1 through 20. Each book may be introduced to the entire group or to smaller groups of children—for example, as a center activity.

Be sure to preread each Little Book before presenting it to children. Many of the books for 1 through 10 have a single sentence spanning several pages; read the text on these pages as a sentence. Books 11 through 20 contain several phrases and sentences; use the periods to help phrase the text when reading aloud. When you are ready to introduce a Little Book, tell children that you have a Little Book for the number 1, for example, and tell them that they will later be given a copy to read, count with, and keep and use at home. Plan to spend 5 to 10 minutes with each book.

Preparing the Little Books in This Resource for Use

Notice that pages for two Little Books appear on each page in the Little Books sections of this resource. This format allows easy photocopying and assembly of the teacher's and children's copies. By photocopying a set of six full pages, two Little Books will be formed in the correct sequence. Remember to make at least one set of Little Books as a group copy for introduction of the books and one copy for each child, if possible.

To prepare the copies, follow these instructions.

1. Remove six perforated pages, which form two complete books, or press the book flat on the copier and copy the six pages.

2. To make more copies of these two Little Books, use these perforated pages or the copied pages as your master, and then copy and collate.

vi

3. Cut the pages horizontally, resulting in two complete books.

4. Staple the left side on each book twice.

You may wish to make an enlarged group copy if you are introducing the Little Book to a group. Laminating this copy will make it sturdier.

Adding some color to the group copy (highlighting pens work well) adds to the visual appeal of the books.

Using the Books

Opening

Arrange the children in front of you, in a semicircle if the group is small or in rows if the group is large. Hold the Little Book so that everyone can see it; making an enlarged group copy will make this easier. Begin the lesson by showing the children the cover page and saying that you will be helping them to read a book for the number 1 (for example). Then say "This book's title is 'My Little Book About 1'" and then underline each use of the numeral with your finger as you read. (You may wish to trace the numeral with your finger.)

Modeling and Tryouts

Read the text aloud to the children in a clear and animated voice. Use your finger to underline the print as you read. After reading the last page, count the pictures together. If after the first reading the children have comments or questions about the numbers or words in the book, be sure to respond in a positive manner.

Then read through the book a second time, again using your voice to animate the brief text, letting the children read the story with you. If you hear words that do not match the text, you may need to model those words again.

In a third reading, have the children (individually or by row) read a page of the Little Book. Read the last page as a group and count the pictured objects. (Reread as often as necessary to help the children become familiar with the text.)

Closing

Conclude each presentation of a Little Book with a reminder that the book is about the number 1, for example. You may want to talk about other experiences with that number or reread a number book already introduced in class.

As you end a session, remind children where the new book will be placed in the classroom so that they can look at it and read it later. Also remind them of your procedure for taking home a copy of the Little Book.

Teacher Tips

1. While accurate reciting of the text is desirable, the children's practice with counting and understanding of number is most important.

2. Be sure to make available to the children, in the reading corner, math center, or other prominent location, a group copy of all introduced Little Books. Children may then enjoy and practice reading these books along with other books.

3. Coloring the books that the children take home can be an in-class or an at-home activity.

4. If possible, provide each child with a personal copy of each of the Little Books to use at home. Children will enjoy reciting the books and counting the pictured objects at home.

5. Give the children suggestions about how to keep their books in one place at home. Another option is to provide them with a special bag with handles or help them to create a decorated box for their Little Books.

6. Introducing parents to the goals and purpose of *Little Books 1, 2, 3* is helpful. A sample parent letter is provided on the next page. Be sure that parents realize that the books are meant primarily for practice with counting and recognizing the associated numeral.

7. Following "My Little Book About 20," you will find two additional special Little Books called "Fun in the Sun" and "In the Playroom." Text is provided and children should draw their own pictures to go along with it. Check that children draw the correct number of items for each page. You may want to introduce these two books by illustrating a copy of each yourself and reading and showing them to the children.

   Have children color the title pages of these books, and add additional art to them if they wish. They should also write their names on the title page after "Pictures by."

   Reread these books with children, just as you would with other Little Books.

Date

Dear Parent/Guardian:

During the year your child will be bringing home Little Books about numbers. These books are for your child to keep and use at home. Please help your child find a special bag or box in which to keep the Little Books.

The brief text and matching pictures in the Little Books will help your child remember and recite the words; your child is not expected to actually read the words. These books are intended to be an enjoyable at-home practice of counting and understanding number.

As you enjoy the books together, answer questions your child may have about the words or numbers, but remember the most important use of the books is practice with counting and recognizing numerals.

Sincerely,

x

Numbers 1-20
Reproducible Little Books

My
Little
Book
About

My
Little
Book
About

1 baby.

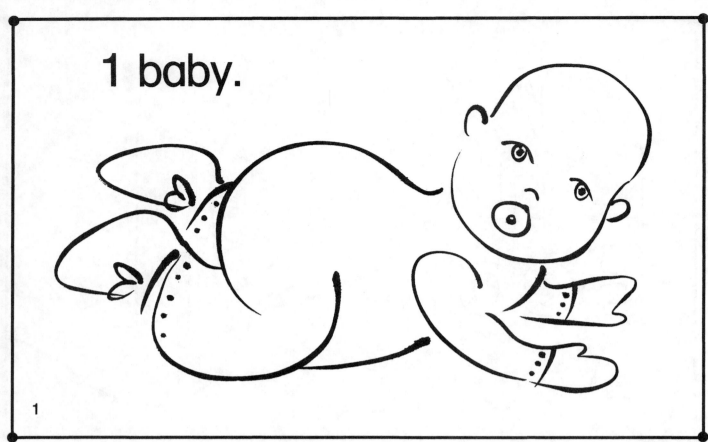

1

2 socks.

1

1 balloon.

2

2 shoes.

2

1 cake

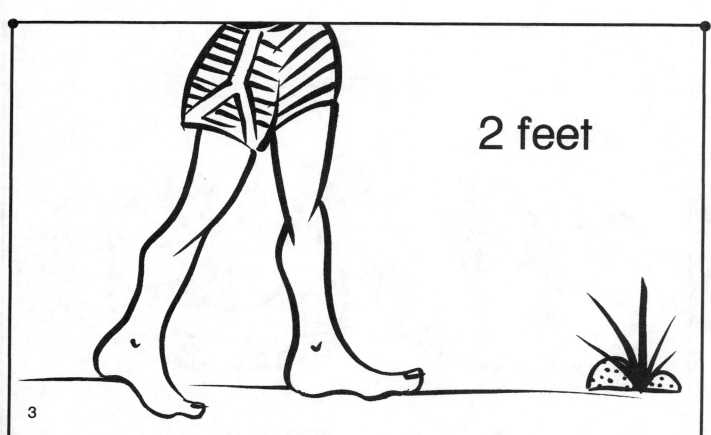

2 feet

with 1 candle.

4

in socks and shoes.

4

I can
count 1
birthday cake.

5

I can
count 2 feet.

5

My
Little
Book
About 3

My
Little
Book
About 4

3 birds.

1

4 frogs.

1

3 bees.

2

4 frogs on a log.

2

3 bees by me.

4 frogs

Fly away bees!

4

catch 4 bugs.

4

1

2

3

I can count 3 bees.

1

2

3

4

I can count 4 frogs.

My
Little
Book
About

5

My
Little
Book
About

6

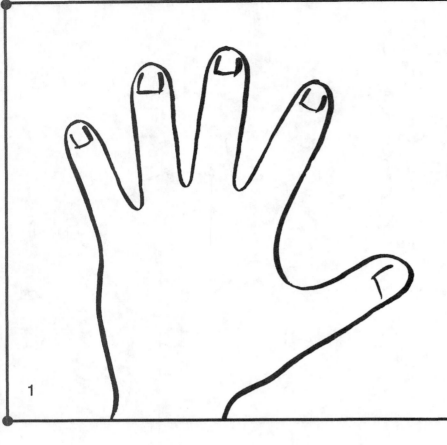

5 fingers.

1

6 stars.

1

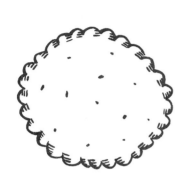

5 cookies.

2

6 cars
with stars.

2

5 children.

3

3

6 cars stop

It's snack time!

4

for 6 children.

4

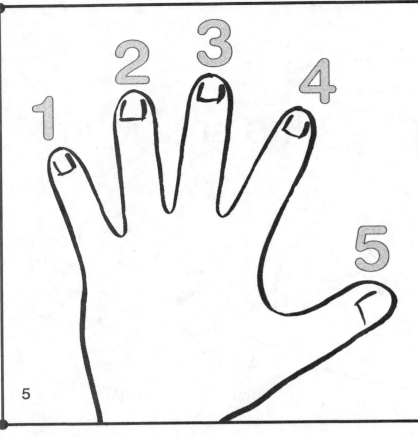

I can count
5 fingers.

I can count
6 cars.

My
Little
Book
About

My
Little
Book
About

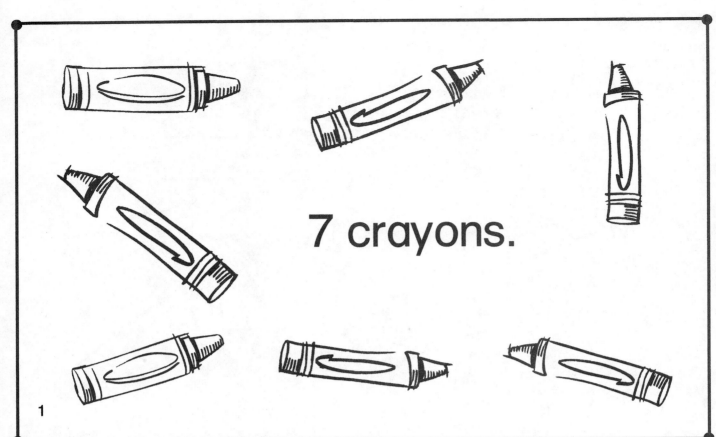

7 crayons.

1

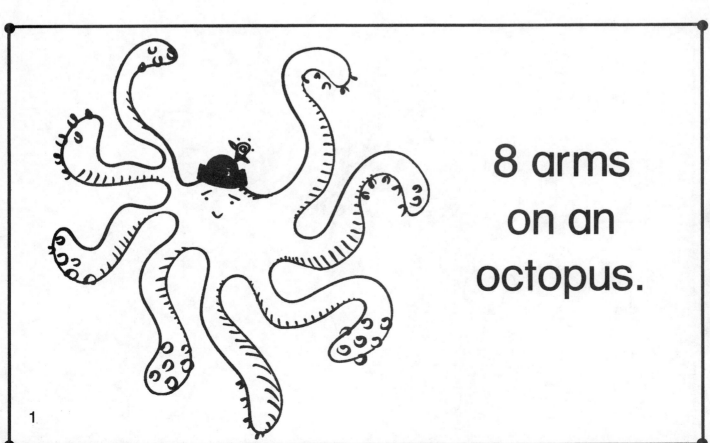

8 arms on an octopus.

1

7 hearts.

2

8 legs on
a spider.

2

One says
"I love you."

8 spiders.

It's for you,
Mommy.

4

8 wait
on a web.

4

1 2 3 4

7

5 6

I can count
7 hearts.

5

1 2 3 4

I can count 8 spiders.

5 6 7 8

5

My
Little
Book
About

9

My
Little
Book
About

10

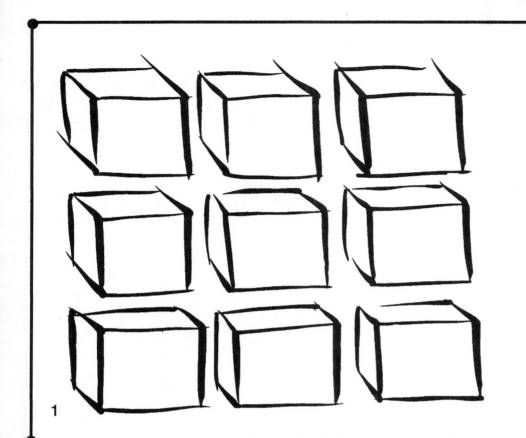

9 boxes.

1

10 toes.

1

5 Xs

2

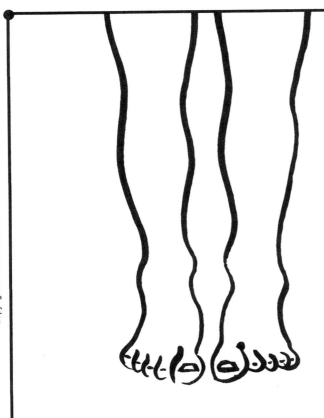

10 toes
on tiptoe.

2

and 4 Os.

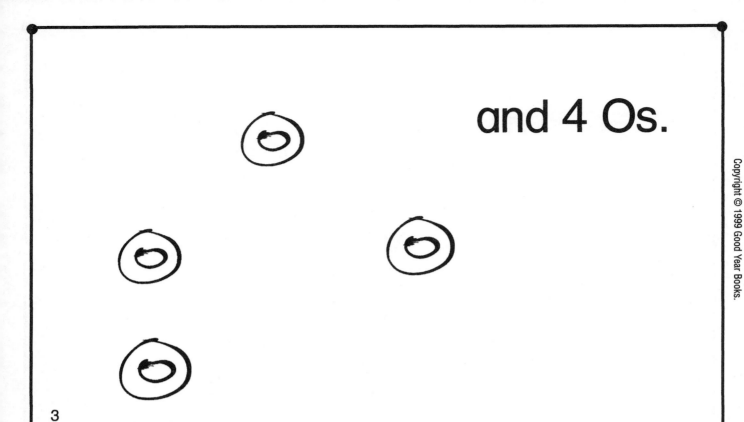

3

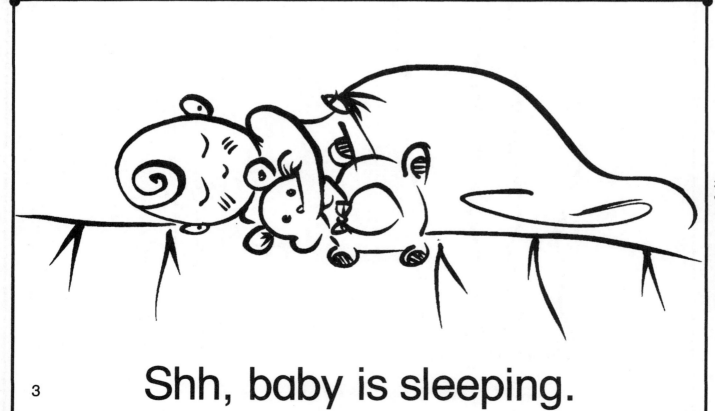

3

Shh, baby is sleeping.

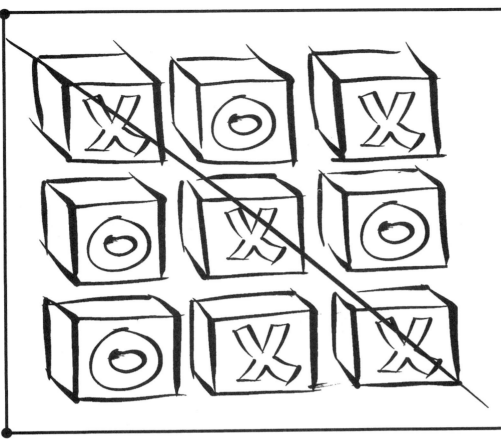

It's tic-tac-toe!

4

Oh-oh, baby wakes up.

4

I can
count 9
Xs and Os.

5

I can count baby's 10 toes.

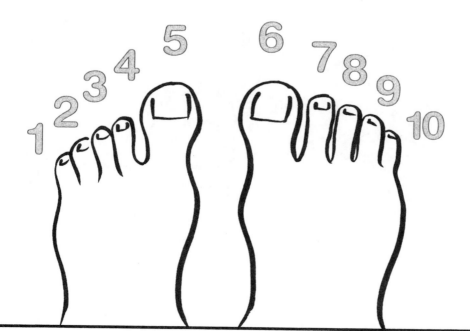

5

My Little Book About

11

My Little Book About

12

11 flowers.

1

12 jars of jam.

1

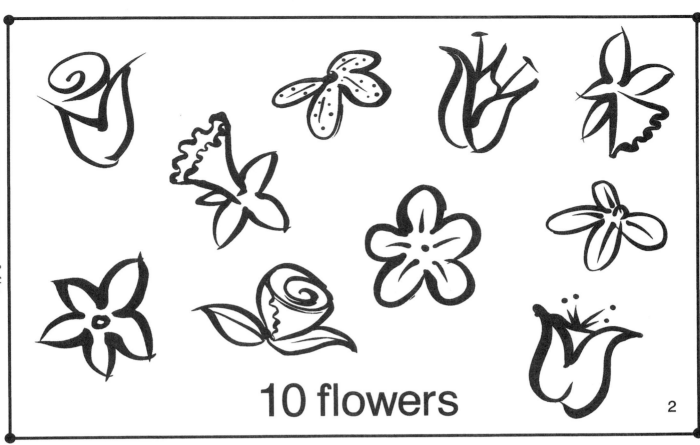

10 flowers

2

10 jars of berry jam

2

and 1
more flower.

3

and 2 jars
of cherry jam.

3

11 flowers in my garden.

4

---

12 jars
for toast.

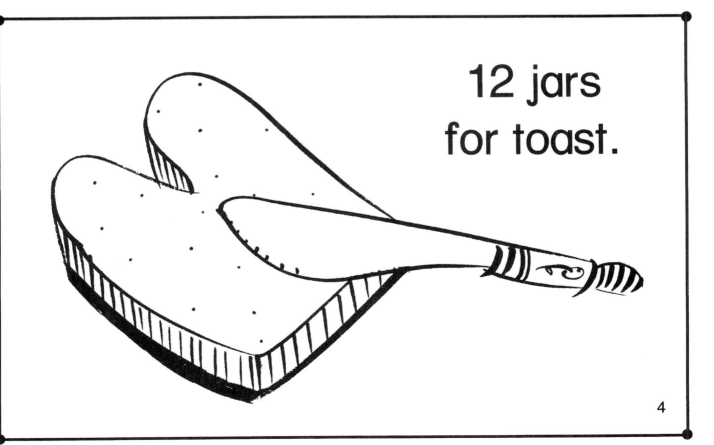

4

I can count 11 flowers.

5

I can count 12 jars of jam.

5

My
Little
Book
About
13

My
Little
Book
About
14

13 ladybugs.

1

14 seashells.

1

  # 10 ladybugs

2

10 shells

2

and 3 more
ladybugs

3

and 4
more shells

3

sit on a sunflower.

4

on the seashore.

4

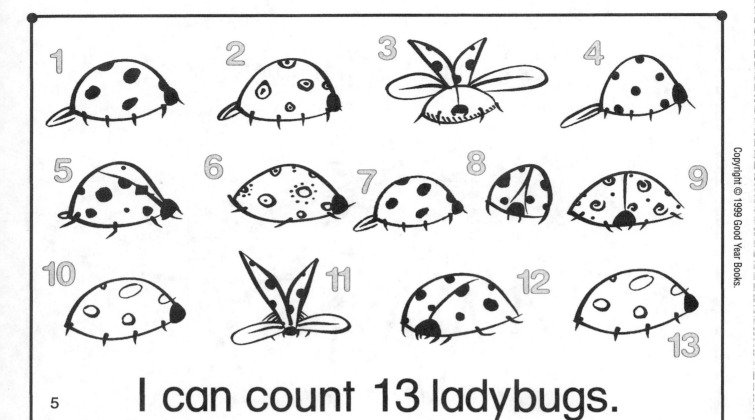

I can count 13 ladybugs.

5

I can count
14 shells.

5

My Little Book About 15

My Little Book About 16

15 balloons.

1

16 pennies.

1

10 for you

2

10 pennies in this hand

2

and 5 for me.

3

and 6 pennies in this hand.

3

Oh-oh! 15 float away.

4

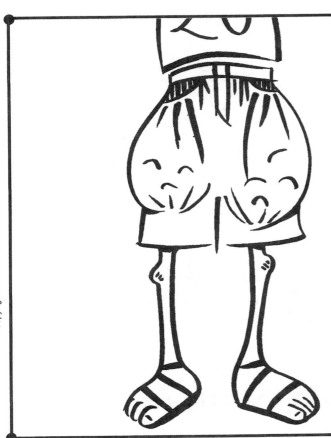

Pockets full of pennies.

4

I can count 15 balloons.

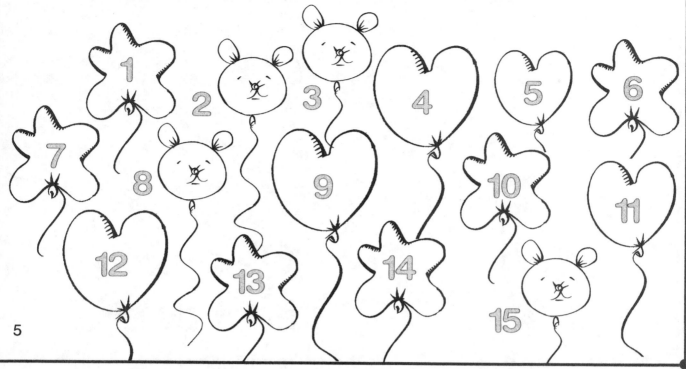

I can count 16 pennies.

My
Little
Book
About

17

My
Little
Book
About

18

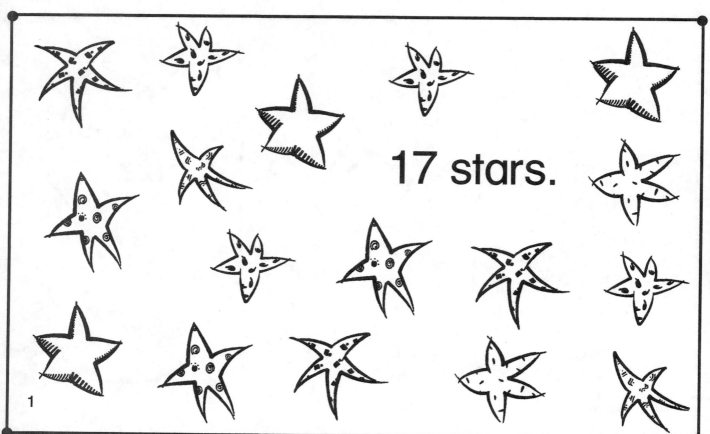

17 stars.

1

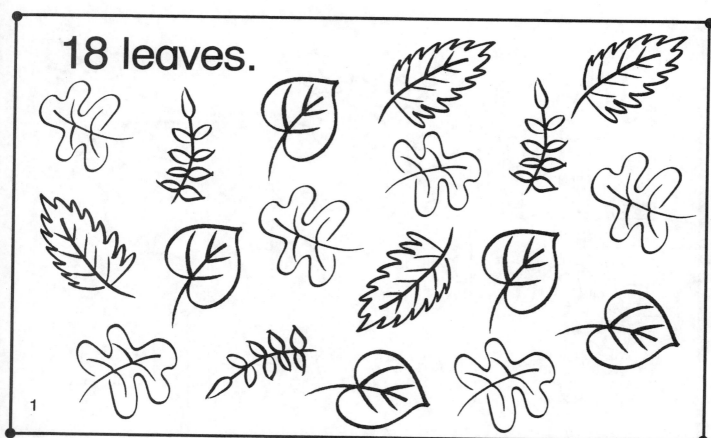

18 leaves.

1

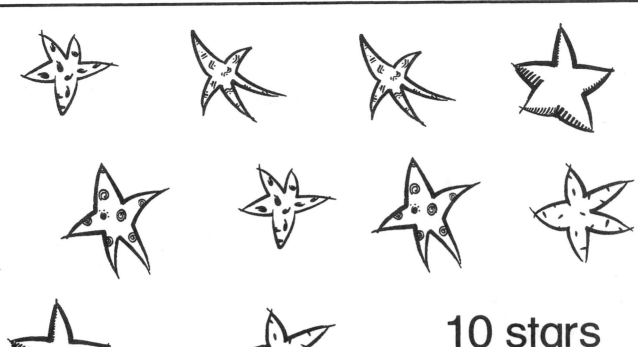

10 stars

2

10 leaves

2

and 7
more stars

3

---

and 8
more leaves

3

twinkle in
the sky.

4

fall from
the tree.

4

I can count 17 stars.

1 2 3 4 5 6 7 8 9 10 11 12 13 14 15 16 17

5

I can count 18 leaves.

1 2 3 4 5 6 7 8 9 10 11 12 13 14 15 16 17 18

5

My Little Book About 19

My Little Book About 20

19 blocks.

1

20 toes.

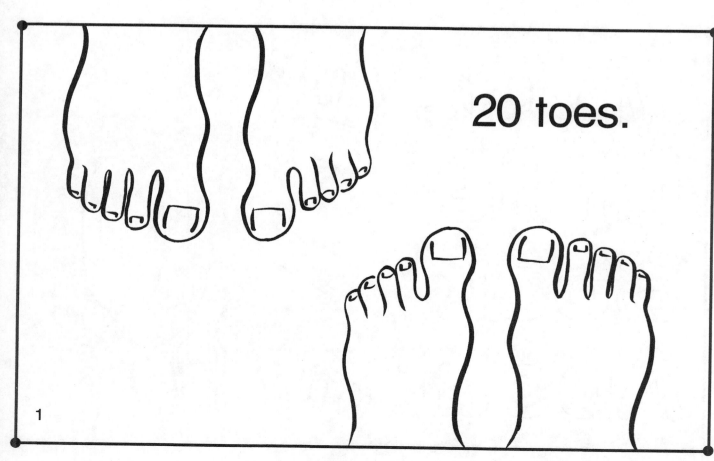

1

10 blocks

2

10 toes

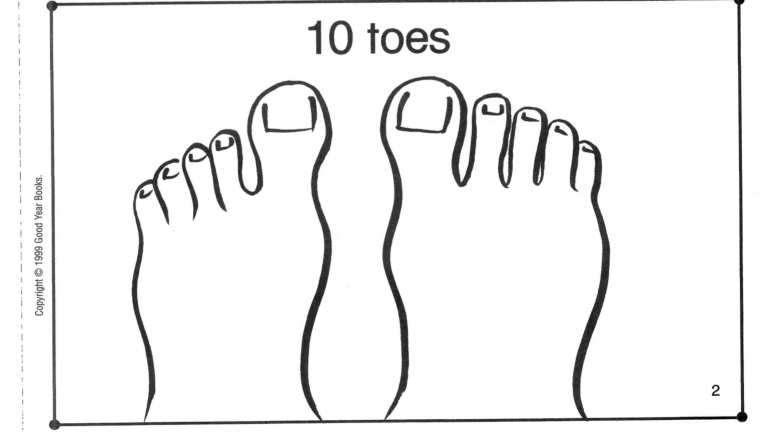

2

and 9
more blocks

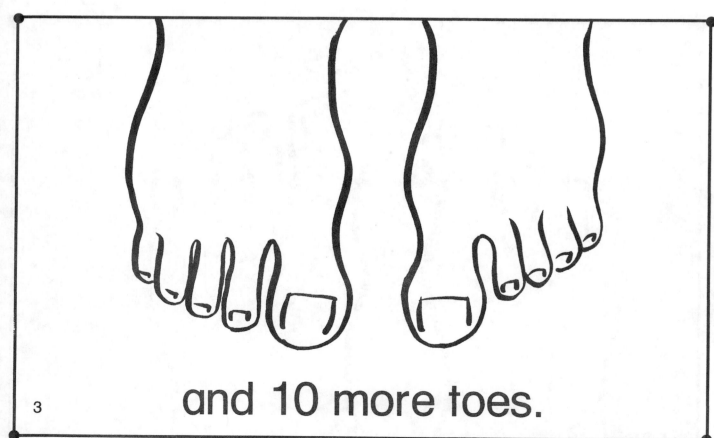

and 10 more toes.

make a very tall tower!

4

20 toes in the sand.

4

I can count 19 blocks.

I can count 20 toes.

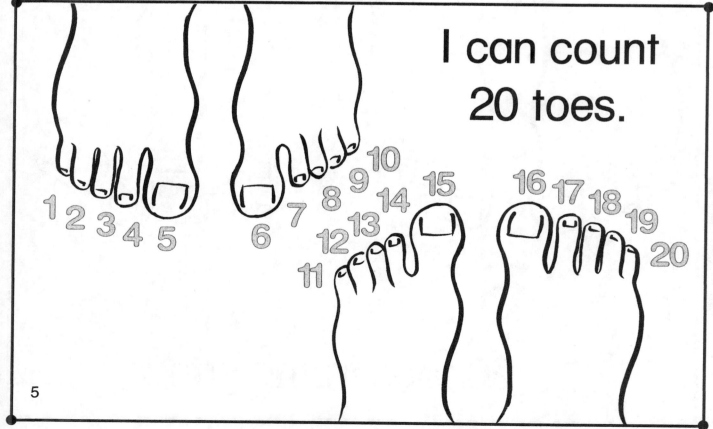

Be the Illustrator!
Reproducible Little Books

Fun in the Sun

Pictures by _____

In the Playroom

Pictures by _____

1 sun.

1

2 trucks.

1

2 slides.

2

4 dolls.

2

3 trees.

3

6 books.

3

4 children.

4

8 puppets.

4

Here I am in the park.

5

This is me and my favorite toy.

5